Music Minus One Trombone

Ballads
FOR
Trombone
WITH
Orchestra

Ballads
FOR
Trombone
WITH
Orchestra

CONTENTS

All songs transcribed and engraved by Robert Edwards

ISBN 978-1-941566-85-5

MMO 3990

All The Way

Word and music by
Jimmy Van Heusen and Sammy Cahn

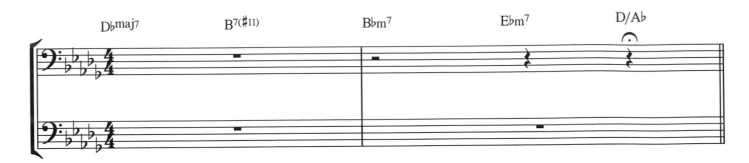

When some bo - dy loves you it's no good un - til he loves you___ all the way.

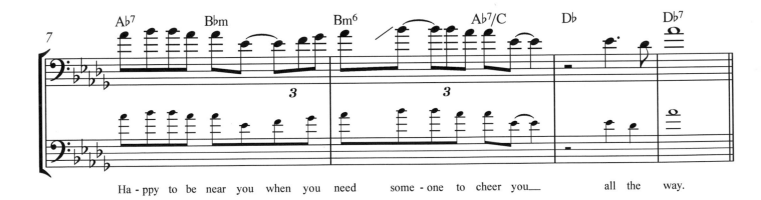

Ha - ppy to be near you when you need some - one to cheer you___ all the way.

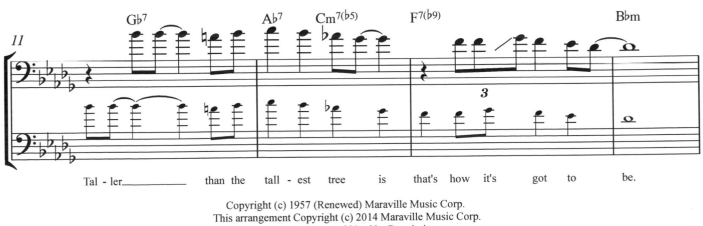

Tal - ler_____ than the tall - est tree is that's how it's got to be.

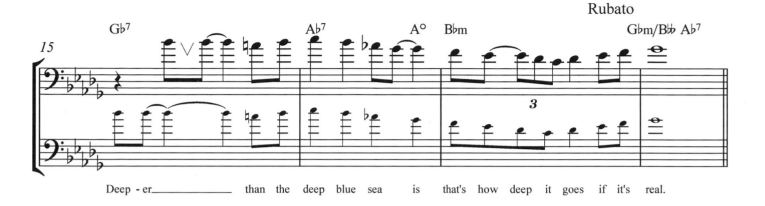

Deep - er_____ than the deep blue sea is that's how deep it goes if it's real.

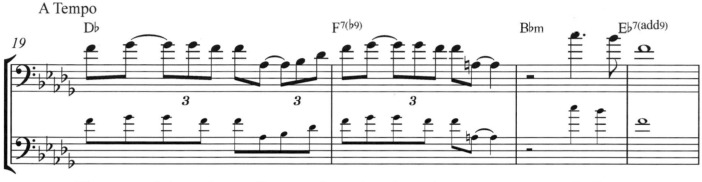

When some - body needs you it's no good un - less she needs you_____ all the way.

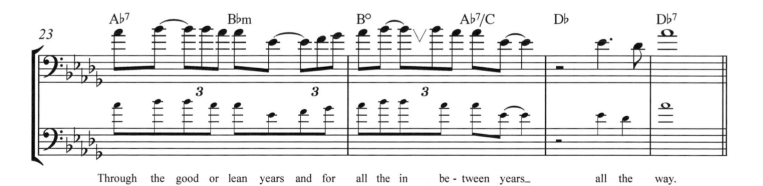

Through the good or lean years and for all the in be - tween years_ all the way.

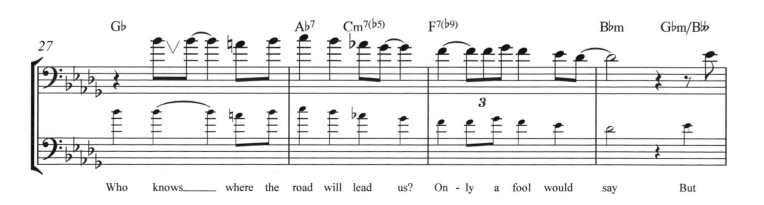

Who knows_____ where the road will lead us? On - ly a fool would say But

if you'll let me love you it's for sure I'm gon - na love you___ all the way.

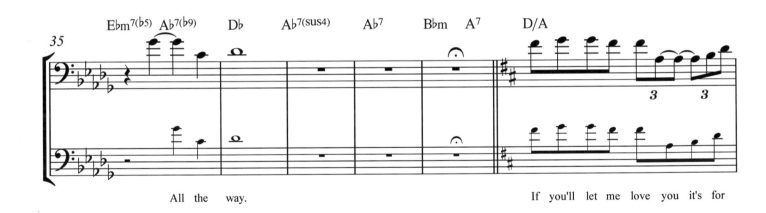

All the way.   If you'll let me love you it's for

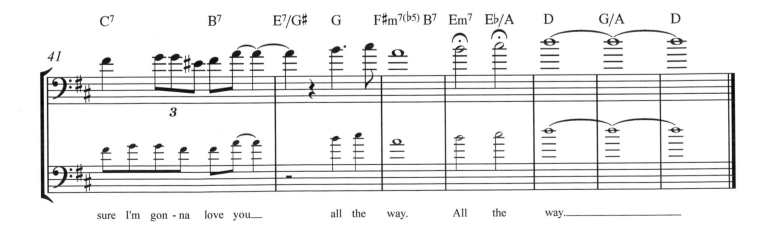

sure I'm gon - na love you___ all the way. All the way._____

This page left blank to facilitate page turns

MMO 3990

I Have Dreamed

Words and music by
Richard Rodgers and Oscar Hammerstein III

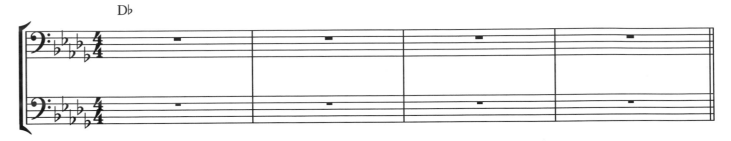

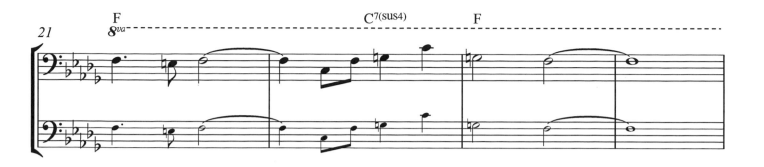

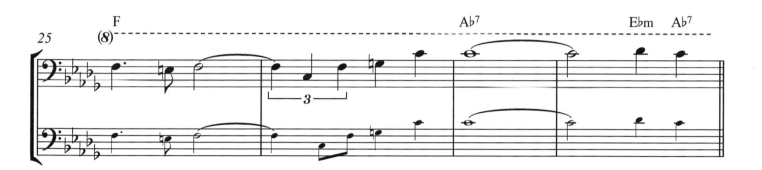

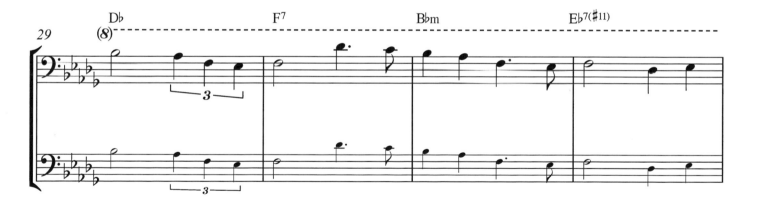

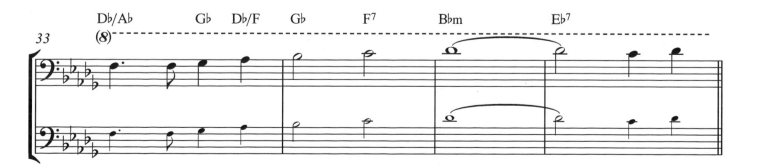

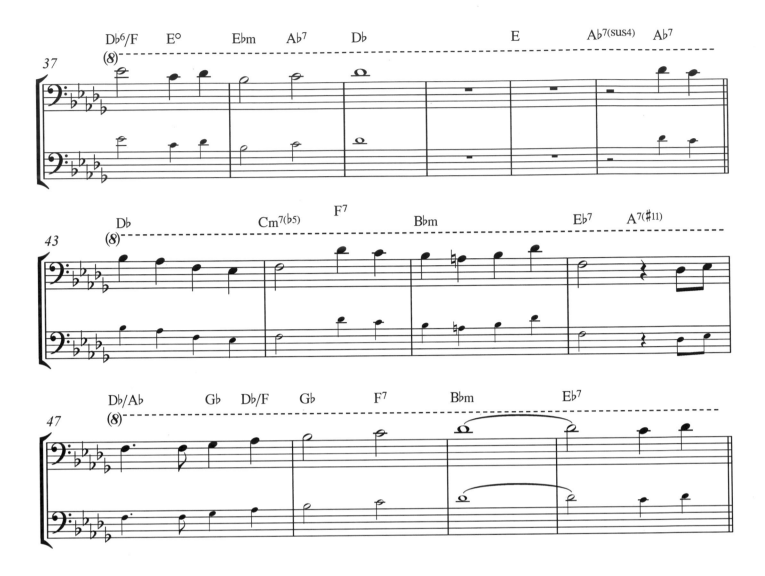

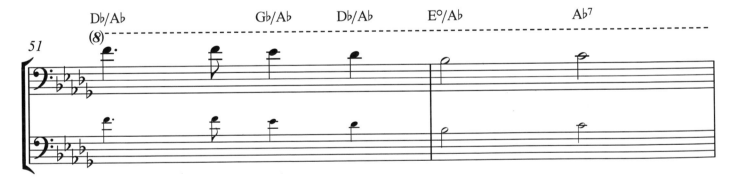

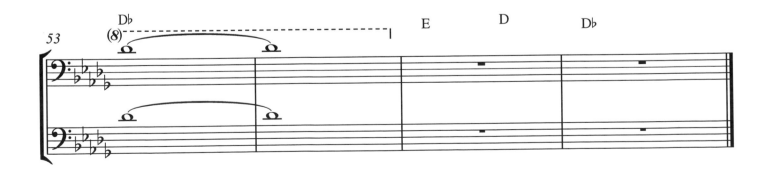

This page left blank to facilitate page turns

I'll Never Be The Same

Music and lyrics by
Gus Khan, Matt Malneck and Frank Signorelli

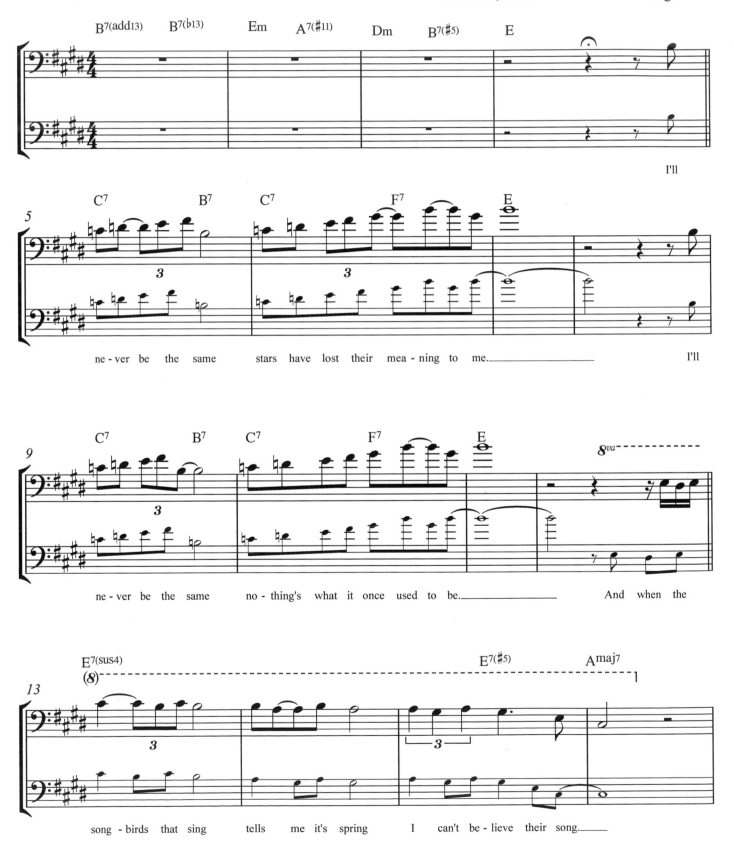

MMO 3990

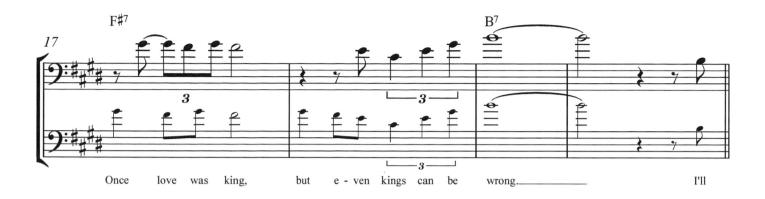

Once love was king, but e-ven kings can be wrong._____ I'll

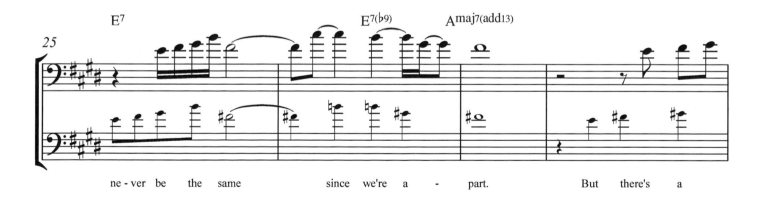

ne-ver be the same there is such a ache in my heart._____ I'll

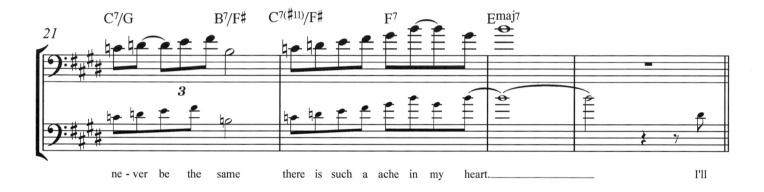

ne-ver be the same since we're a - part. But there's a

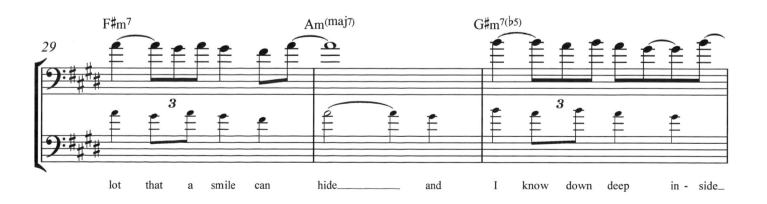

lot that a smile can hide_____ and I know down deep in-side_____

14

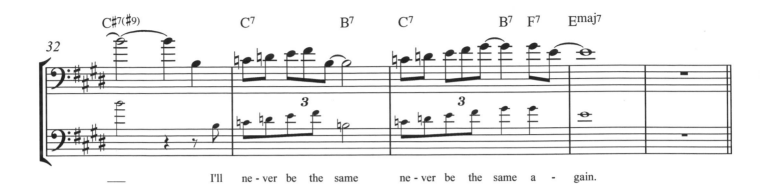

I'll ne - ver be the same   ne - ver be the same a - gain.

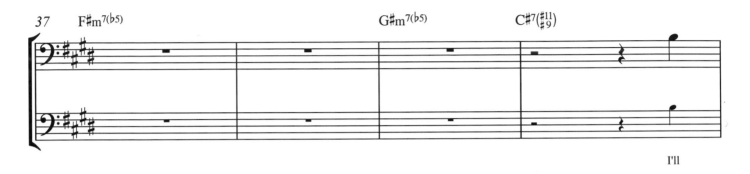

I'll

Rubato   A Tempo

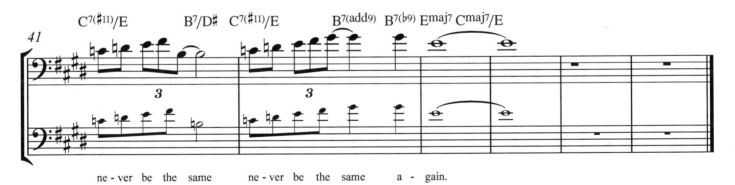

ne - ver be the same   ne - ver be the same   a - gain.

OTHER GREAT TROMBONE EDITIONS FROM MUSIC MINUS ONE

Chamber Classics
____Art of Improvisation (Dorian mode) Vol.1 ....MMO CD 7005
____Art of Improvisation (Mixolydian mode) Vol.2 ....MMO CD 7006
____Baroque Brass and Beyond: (Illinojs Brass)..MMO CD 3904
____Big Band Ballads Tenor or Bass Trombone(G. Roberts) ....MMO CD 3907
____Classical Trombone Solos ....MMO CD 3909
____Music for Brass Ensemble..MMO CD 3905
____Sticks & Bones: Brass Quintets...MMO CD 3927
____STRAVINSKY L'Histoire du Soldat ....MMO CD 3908

Instrumental Classics with Orchestra
____Band Aids: Concert Band Favorites..MMO CD 3930
____Popular Concert Favorites w/Orch ....MMO CD 3929

Jazz, Standards and Big Band
____2+2=5: A Study Odd Times ....MMO CD 2044
____Adventures in N.Y. & Chicago Jazz (Bobby Gordon) ....MMO CD 3923
____Bacharach Revisited (Big Band + Strings) ....MMO CD 3974
____Back to Basics - Style of the Basie Band (Peter Ecklund) ....MMO CD 3985
____Ballads with Orchestra, Ira Nepus, soloist...MMO CD 3943
____Big Band Ballads: Tenor/ Bass Trombone(George Roberts) ....MMO CD 3907
____Chicago-Style Jam Session Evan Christopher) ....MMO CD 3921
____Classic Ballads with Orchestra, Ira Nepus..MMO CD 3943
____Classic Standards for Trombone & Orch (Alan Kaplan) ....MMO CD 3990
____From Dixie to Swing (Davern,Dickenson,Cheatham) ....MMO CD 3926
____Great Ballads with Orchestra (Alan Kaplan, trombone) ....MMO CD 3995
____Isle of Orleans (Tim Laughlin N.O.Jazz Band)...MMO CD 3933
____Jazz Standards w/Strings (All Star Rhythm Section) ....MMO CD 3910
____Motown Trombone, Ira Nepus, soloist ....MMO CD 3936
____New Orleans Classics (Tim Laughlin N.O.Jazz Band)....................................MMO CD 3934
____Northern Lights (Canadian All Star Band) ....MMO CD 2004
____PCH Pacific Coast Horns, vol. 1: Longhorn Serenade ....MMO CD 3975
____PCH Pacific Coast Horns, vol. 2: 76 Trombones and other favs (Int-Adv) ....MMO CD 3976
____PCH Pacific Coast Horns, V.3: Where Trombone Reigns ....MMO CD 3977
____Play Ballads w/a Band (Bob Wilber All Star Band) ....MMO CD 3972
____Standards for Trombone (Ira Lepus, trombone) ....MMO CD 3935
____Studio City ....MMO CD 2024
____Swing with a Band (Milton DeLugg Band)..MMO CD 3973
____Take One Jersey City College Band ....MMO CD 2014
____Unsung Hero: Sinatra Standards Tenor/Bass Trombone (Geo.Roberts) ....MMO CD 3906

Laureate Master Series Concert Solos
____Beginning Solos, v. I (Brevig) ....MMO CD 3911
____Beginning Solos, v. II (Friedman)...MMO CD 3912
____Int. Solos, v. I (Brown)...MMO CD 3913
____Int. Solos, v. II (Friedman) ....MMO CD 3914
____Advanced Solos, v. I (Brown) ....MMO CD 3915
____Advanced Solos, v. II (Brevig) ....MMO CD 3916
____Advanced Solos, v. III (Brown) ....MMO CD 3917
____Advanced Solos, v. IV (Friedman) ....MMO CD 3918
____Advanced Solos, v. V (Brevig) ....MMO CD 3919

Student Series
____Classic Themes: 27 Easy Songs (Harriet Wingreen) ....MMO CD 3932
____Easy Jazz Duets (Benny Goodman Rhythm Section)....................................MMO CD 3903
____Easy Solos: Student Level, v. I (Harriet Wingreen) ....MMO CD 3901
____Easy Solos: Student Level, v. II (Harriet Wingreen) ....MMO CD 3902
____Teacher's Partner: Basic Studies ....MMO CD 3920
____12 Classic Jazz Standards (Bryan Shaw, Trpt.) ....MMO CD 7010
____12 More Classic Jazz Standards (Tom Fischer) ....MMO CD 7011
____World Favorites: 41 Easy Pieces (Harriett Wingreen) ....MMO CD 3931

I'm A Fool To Want You

Words and music by
Frank Sinatra, Jack Wolf and Joel Herron

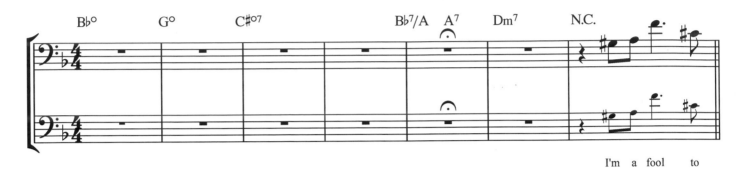

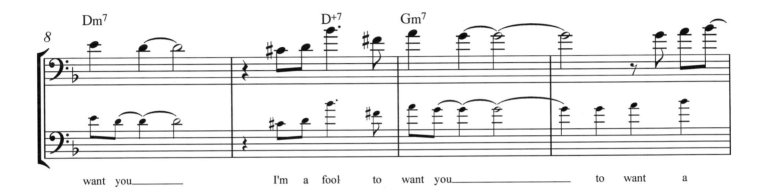

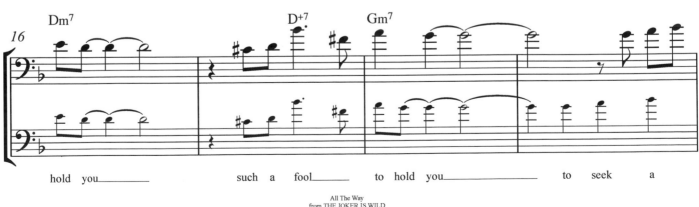

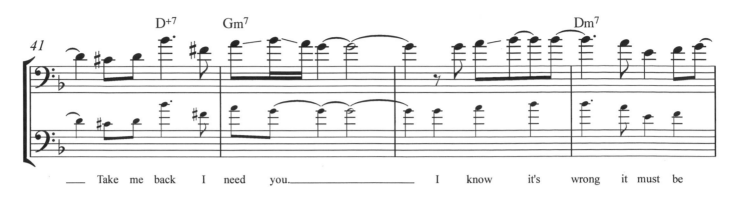

Take me back   I   need   you._____   I   know   it's   wrong   it   must   be

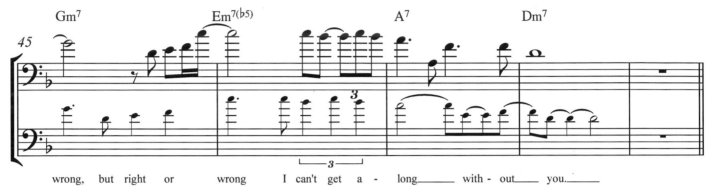

wrong,   but   right   or   wrong   I   can't   get   a - long_____   with - out____   you.____

Time   and   time   a - gain   I   said   I'd   leave   you_____   time   and   time   a -

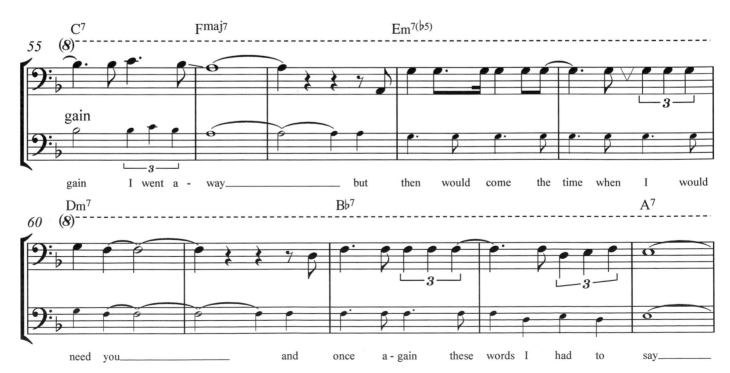

gain   I   went   a - way_____   but   then   would   come   the   time   when   I   would

need   you_____   and   once   a - gain   these   words   I   had   to   say_____

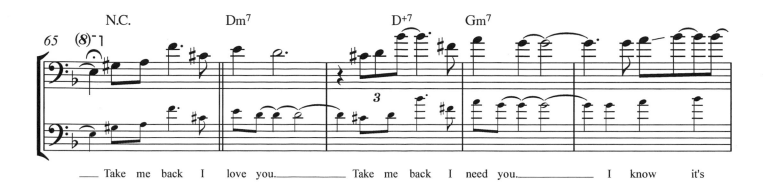

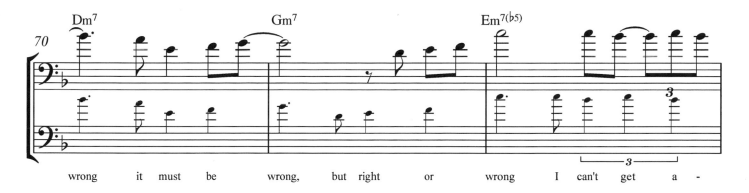

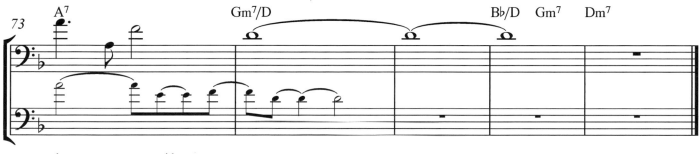

Take me back I love you. Take me back I need you. I know it's

wrong it must be wrong, but right or wrong I can't get a -

long with - out you.

Quiet Nights of Quiet Stars
(Corcovado)

Words and music by
Antonio Carlos Jobim

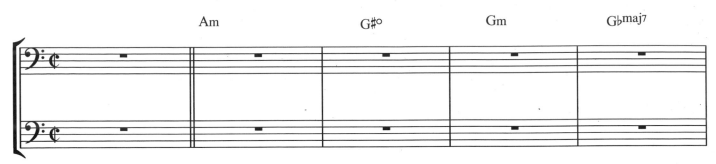

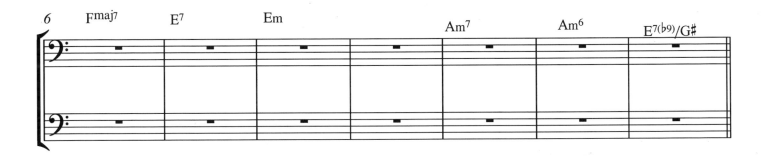

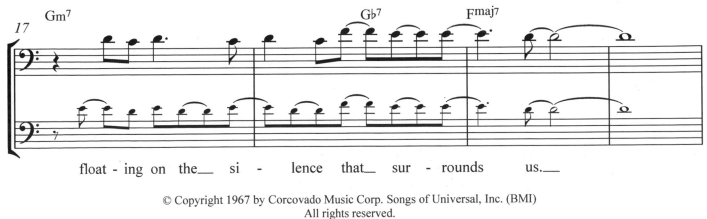

Qui - et nights of__ qui - et__ stars   qui - et chords   from   my__ gui - tar__

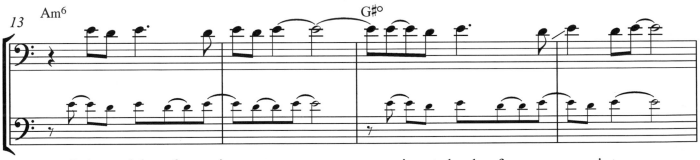

float - ing on the__ si - lence that__ sur - rounds   us.__

Qui - et thoughts and_ qui - et_ dreams,_   qui - et walks by_ qui - et streams

and_ a win- dow_ look - ing_ on_ the moun - tains and the   sea_____ how love - ly._

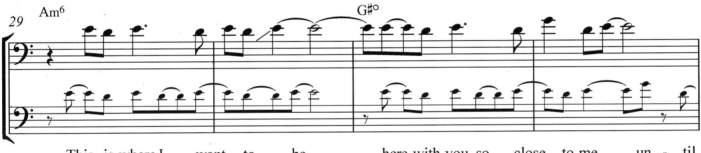

This is where I__ want_ to__ be,   here_with you so_ close_ to me   un - til

__ the fi - nal flick-er of_ life's am - ber._____

I   who_ was lost and lone - ly__   be-liev-ing life was on - ly__

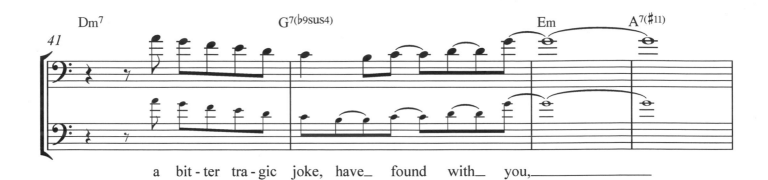

a bit - ter tra - gic joke, have_ found with_ you,_____

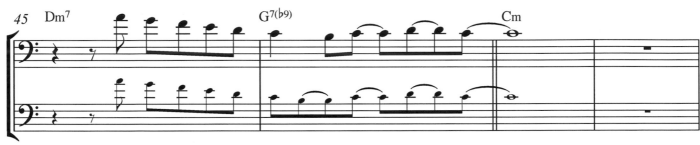

the mean-ing of ex - is- tence_ of___ my___ love.___

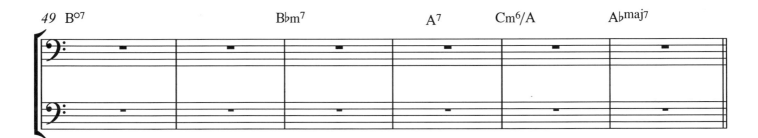

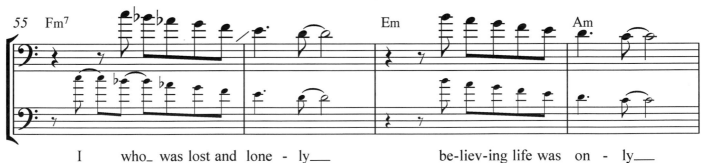

I who_ was lost and lone - ly___ be-liev-ing life was on - ly___

a bit - ter tra - gic joke, have_ found with_ you,_____

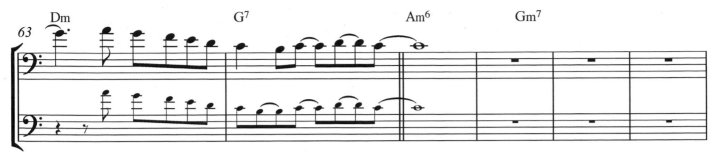

the mean-ing of ex - is tence of__ my_ love.__

It Never Entered My Mind

Words and music by
Richard Rodgers and Lorenz Hart

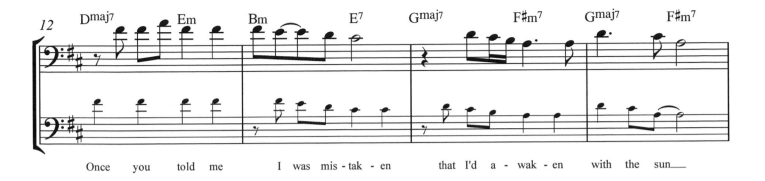

Once you told me I was mis - tak - en that I'd a - wak - en with the sun__

and or - der or - ange juice for one__ it ne - ver en - tered my ming__

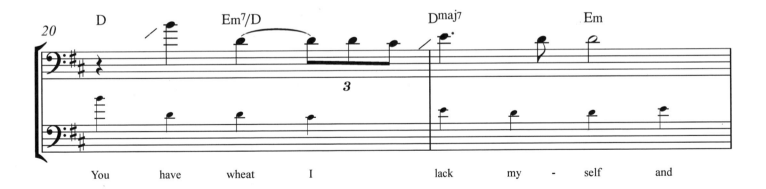

You have wheat I lack my - self and

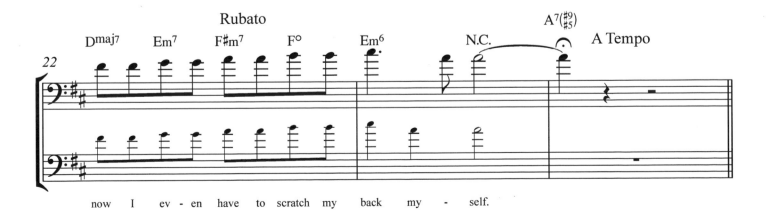

now I ev - en have to scratch my back my - self.

Once you warned me that if you scorn me I'll say a lone - ly prayer a - gain__

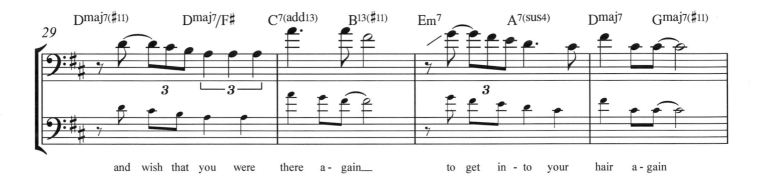

and wish that you were there a - gain__ to get in - to your hair a - gain

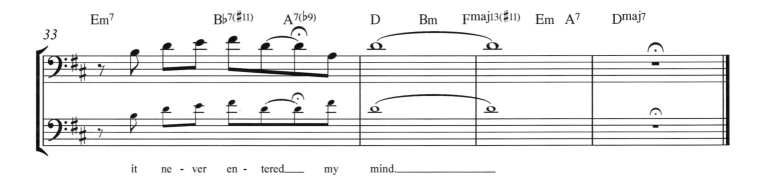

it ne - ver en - tered__ my mind._____

Once Upon A Time

Words and music by
Charles Strous and Lee Adams

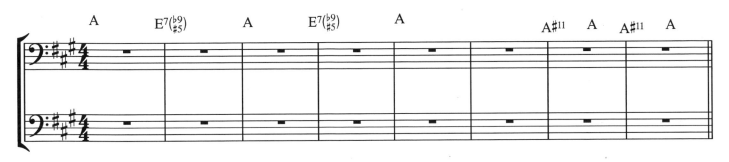

Once u - pon a time_____ a girl with moon - light in here eyes_____

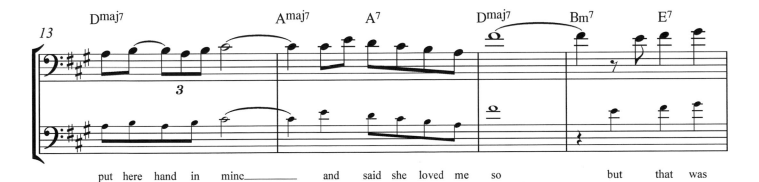

put here hand in mine_____ and said she loved me so but that was

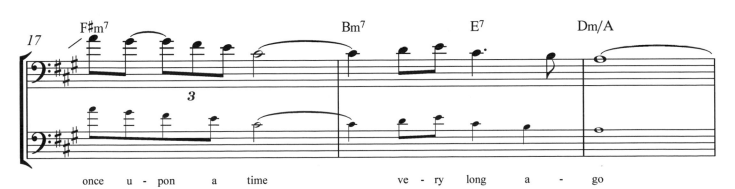

once u - pon a time ve - ry long a - go

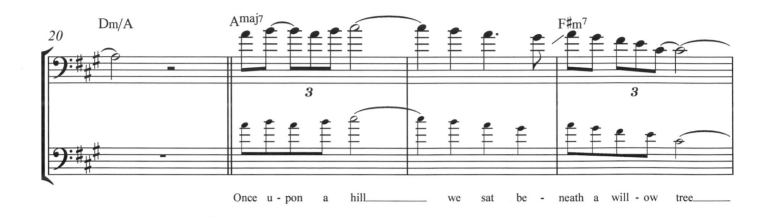

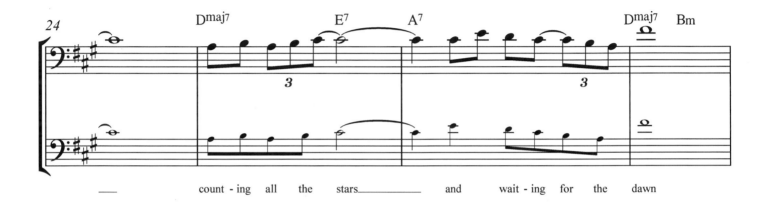

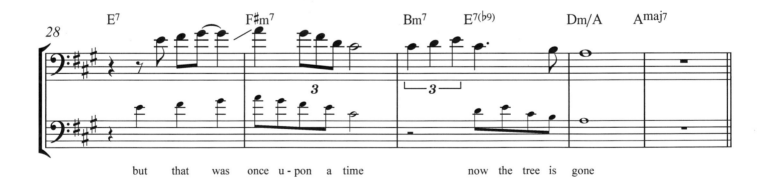

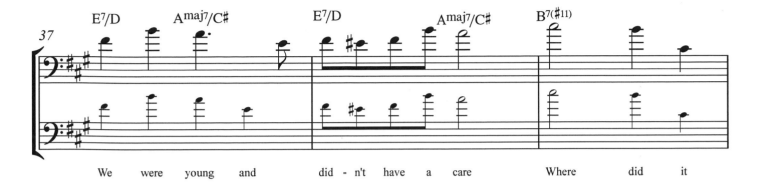

We were young and did-n't have a care Where did it

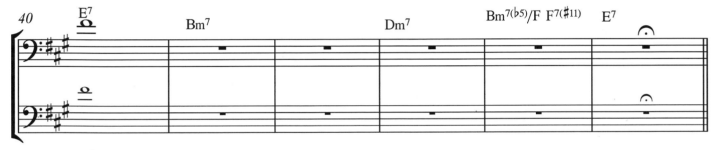

go?

Once u-pon a time_____ the world was sweet-er than you knew_____

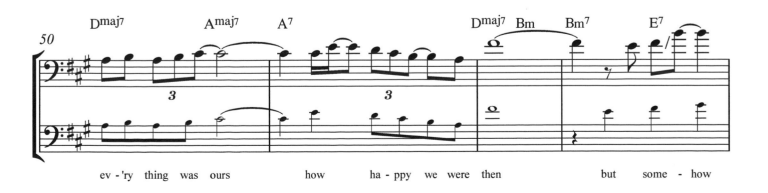

ev-'ry thing was ours how ha-ppy we were then but some-how

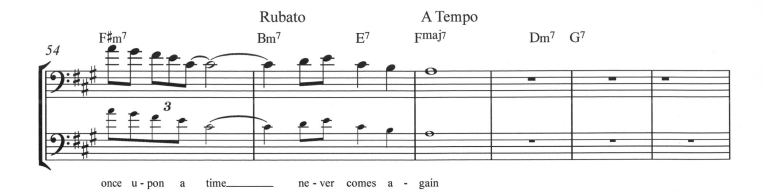

once u - pon a time_____ ne - ver comes a - gain

Once u - pon a time ne - ver comes a - gain.

All Or Nothing At All

Words and music by Cole Porter

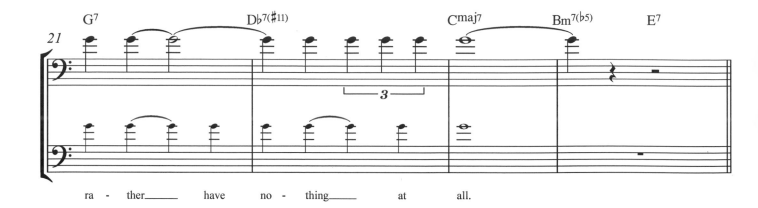

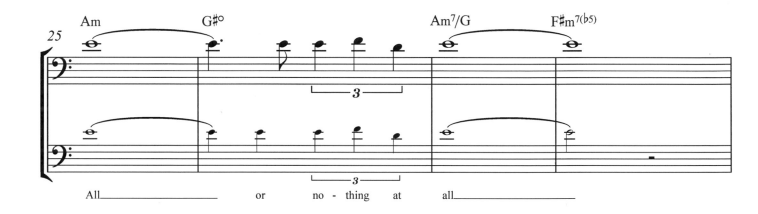

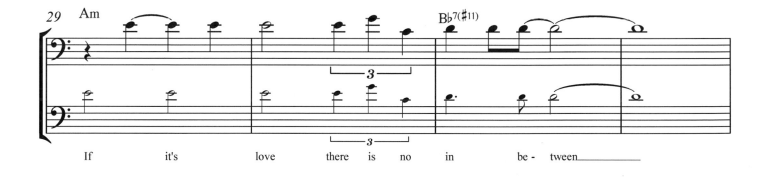

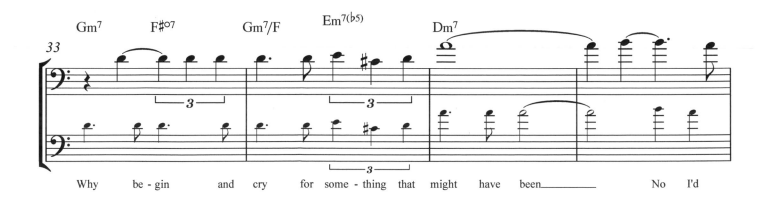

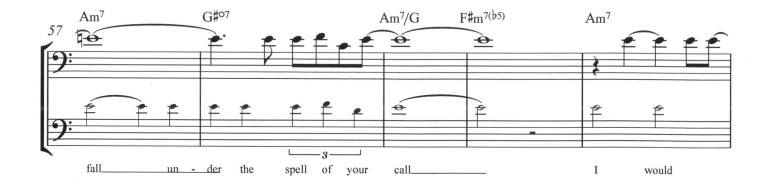

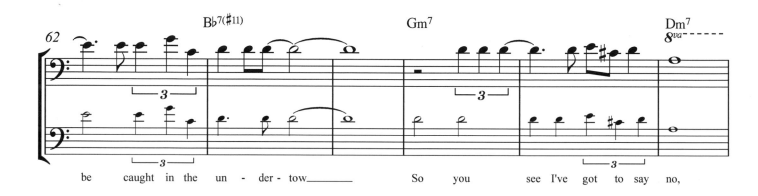

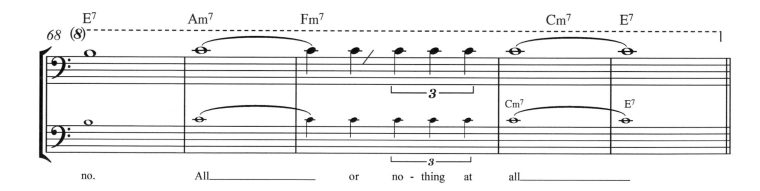

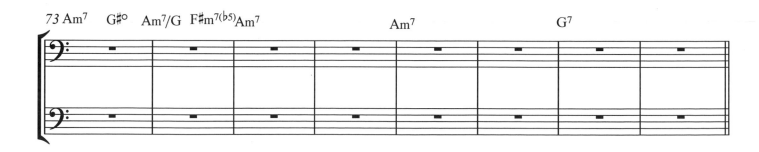

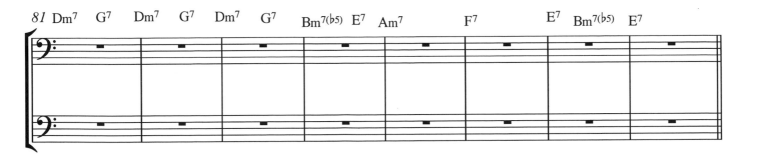

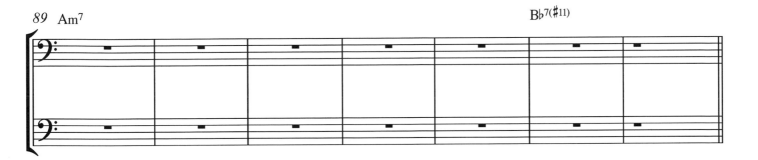

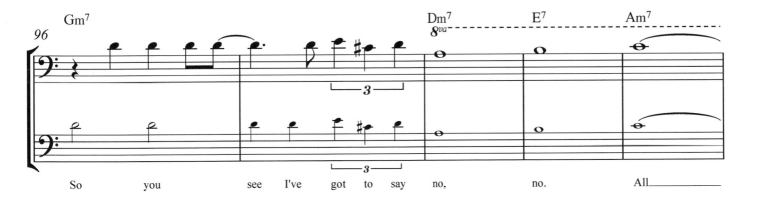

So you see I've got to say no, no. All_____

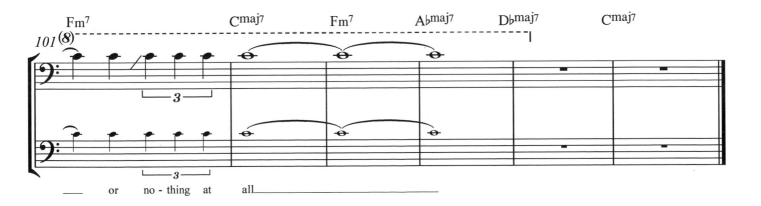

_____ or no-thing at all_____

I'll Be Seeing You

Words and music by
Sammy Fain and Irving Kahal

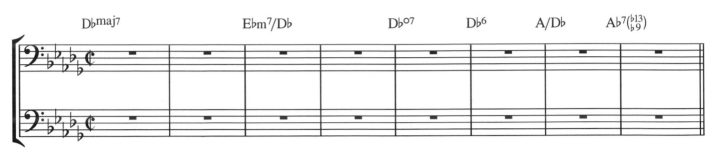

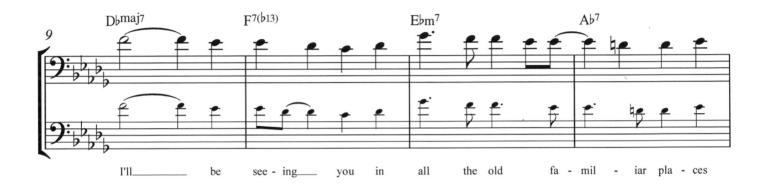

I'll____ be see - ing____ you in all the old fa - mil - iar pla - ces

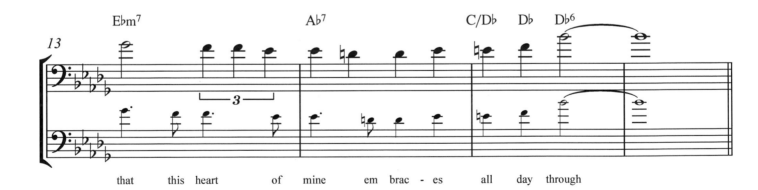

that this heart of mine em brac - es all day through

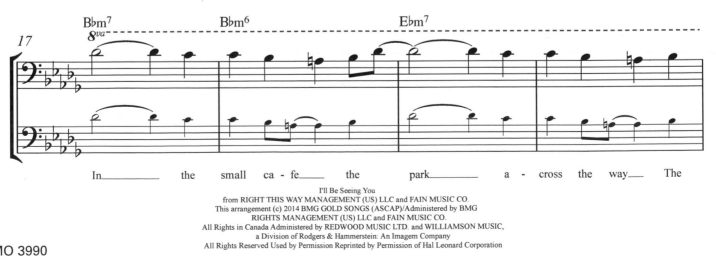

In____ the small ca - fe____ the park____ a - cross the way____ The

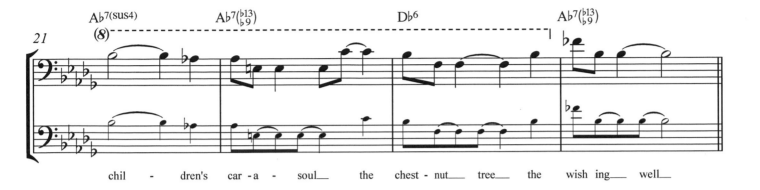

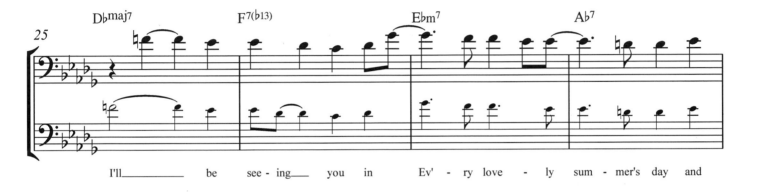

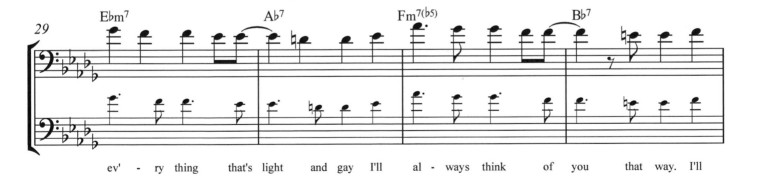

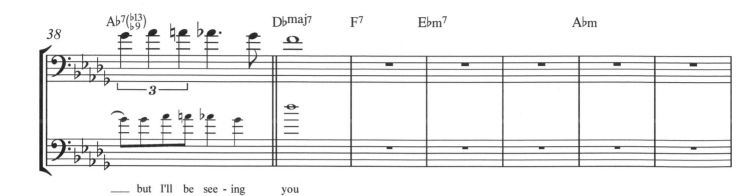

but I'll be see - ing you

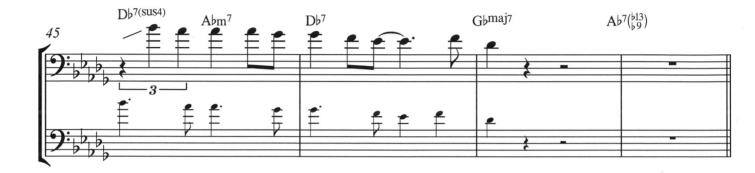

I'll_____ be see ing___ you in Ev' - ry love - ly sum - mer's day and ev' - ry thing that's

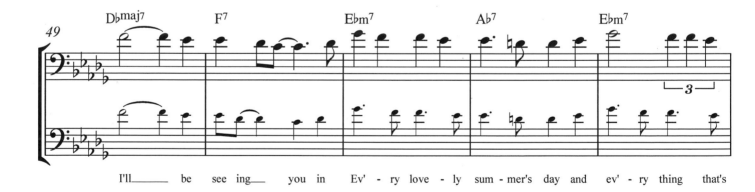

light and gay I'll al - ways think of you that way. I'll find you in the mor - ning sun and

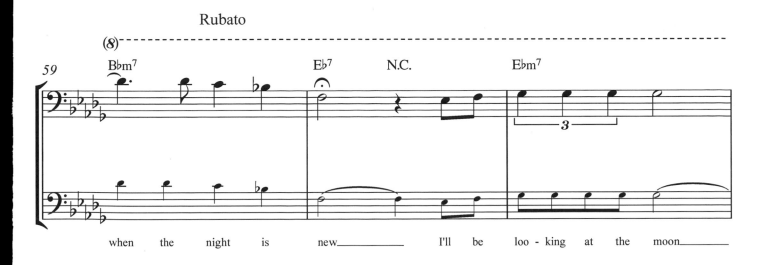

when the night is new_____ I'll be loo - king at the moon_____

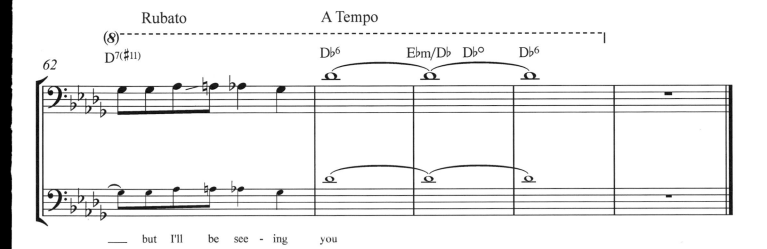

_____ but I'll be see - ing you

Music Minus One
50 Executive Boulevard • Elmsford, New York 10523-1325
914-592-1188 • e-mail: info@musicminusone.com
www.musicminusone.com

MMO 3990

ISBN 978-1-941566-85-5